Unicorns

Magical Creatures from Myth and Fiction

Unicorns
Magical Creatures from Myth and Fiction

GENERAL EDITOR:
MIA DI FRANCESCO

tangerine press®

an imprint of

SCHOLASTIC

www.scholastic.com

an imprint of
SCHOLASTIC
www.scholastic.com

Scholastic and Tangerine Press and associated logos are trademarks of Scholastic Inc.

Published by Tangerine Press, an imprint of Scholastic Inc., 557 Broadway; New York, NY 10012

Scholastic Canada Ltd.
Markham, Ontario

Scholastic Canada Ltd.
Toronto, Ontario

Scholastic Australia Pty. Ltd
Gosford, NSW

Scholastic New Zealand Ltd.
Greenmount, Auckland

Scholastic UK
Coventry, Warwickshire

10 9 8 7 6 5 4 3 2 1

ISBN-13: 978-0-545-01318-5
ISBN-10: 0-545-01318-6

Editorial and design by
Amber Books Ltd
Bradley's Close
74–77 White Lion Street
London N1 9PF
United Kingdom
www.amberbooks.co.uk

Project Editor: Sarah Uttridge
Design: Talking Design
Illustrations: Myke Taylor/The Art Agency

Printed in Singapore

Picture credits: All © Amber Books Ltd.

Contents

Introduction

Today we have grown used to not believing in unicorns. Advances in science and our knowledge of nature have made such creatures seem like nothing more than dreams of an older and more superstitious world. Yet we need to be careful not to dismiss unicorns too quickly. For thousands of years before our present age, stretching back to before 4000 B.C., people of every nation, race, and religion have proclaimed unicorns to be real. In ancient Greece, the natural historian Ctesias, who lived in the 4th century B.C., described one-horned creatures whose horns could be used to treat poisoning. The great philosopher Aristotle (384–322 B.C.) and the Roman writer Pliny (A.D. 23–79) were also convinced of the existence of unicorns. On the other side of the world, Japanese and Chinese legends of unicorns date back as far as 2900 B.C. Great leaders including Julius Caesar and Genghis Khan are thought to have seen unicorns personally.

We can explain many alleged unicorn sightings as common animals. The oryx antelope, for example, has two long, thin horns, but, in profile, only one horn can be seen.

Goats are sometimes born with a deformity that gives them one horn instead of two. Whatever the case, by the medieval period (5th – 16th centuries A.D.), legends and images of the unicorn were everywhere. In this age, unicorns were seen carved into church stonework and decorating stained-glass windows. Whole tapestries were embellished with scenes of unicorn hunts. Paintings depict young maidens cradling unicorns in their laps. Unicorns even grace official royal coats of arms; in the case of the United Kingdom and Canada, these are still in use today. And just in case we think of medieval people as superstitious and too quick to believe, travel writers well into the 18th and even 19th centuries gave eyewitness accounts of unicorns in far-off countries such as India and China.

Unicorns are still with us today in books, art, and from films such as *Legend* to the stories of *Harry Potter*. Why haven't the myths and the stories of unicorns died out by now? For one, in a sometimes dark world, we are spellbound by their purity and goodness, and the tiny possibility that they may still be hidden out there in the most remote corners of our planet. Their magical abilities and great beauty also attract us. Perhaps most important, however, is that by keeping unicorns alive in our imagination, we hope to feel something of the power, grace, and beauty that they have inspired for thousands of years.

Kirin

Body
The kirin has extremely strong muscles to push it forward in a racing gallop. Its strong body is said to be like that of a lion or bull, making the kirin a threatening creature.

Mane
A wild mane can make the kirin look more like an Eastern dragon than a unicorn.

Eyes
The kirin's eyes are penetrating—they can look into a person's soul and see both guilt and innocence.

Horn
The kirin's horn is an instrument of life or death, and so is extremely powerful, sharp, and strong.

N OT ALL UNICORNS ARE GENTLE, LOVING CREATURES. *The fearsome kirin, or sin-you, of Japan had the physique of a mighty bull or lion, a burning gaze, and wild hair. It was typically a shy creature, hiding out in the forests, but it also had the uncanny ability to tell whether a person was guilty of a crime or not. In medieval Japanese folk courts, the judges would call on the kirin to appear. The accused person had to stand in front of the unicorn; if he was guilty, the kirin would charge and run him through with its lethal horn, killing him instantly. The Japanese unicorn was also known as "ikkakujuu." This word means "one horn beast."*

ACTUAL SIZE

▶ THE KIRIN STRIKES DOWN A GUILTY MAN. *In medieval Japan, a man is brought before a court of elders, charged with murder. The court struggles to make its judgment, but at that point a kirin is led into the room. The accused starts to tremble—he knows what is coming. The kirin stares at him with a gaze that seems to burn all the way into his soul. The mysterious animal instantly sees that the man is guilty of the murder, and with a snort of breath charges and drives its knifelike horn into the man's chest.*

Where in the world?

The kirin lived deep in the mountainous forests of Japan. It was a rare creature, and eventually became extinct as more and more of its precious woodland habitat was cut down to make way for people.

JAPAN ●

Did you know?

★ Unicorns used to be honored in ancient Japanese religious rituals. During the ceremonies, the kirin was said to be an animal of both peace and judgment.

★ Japan and China are not the only Far Eastern countries to honor the unicorn. Vietnamese people perform a unicorn dance on a night of the full moon at the beginning of the monsoon season. They wear masks and costumes during the dance to hide their identities.

★ Japanese children are sometimes told legends of the kirin to encourage them never to lie and to behave well even when alone.

★ The kirin is thought to have suffered extinction when humans cut down its forest habitat.

Hunted Unicorns

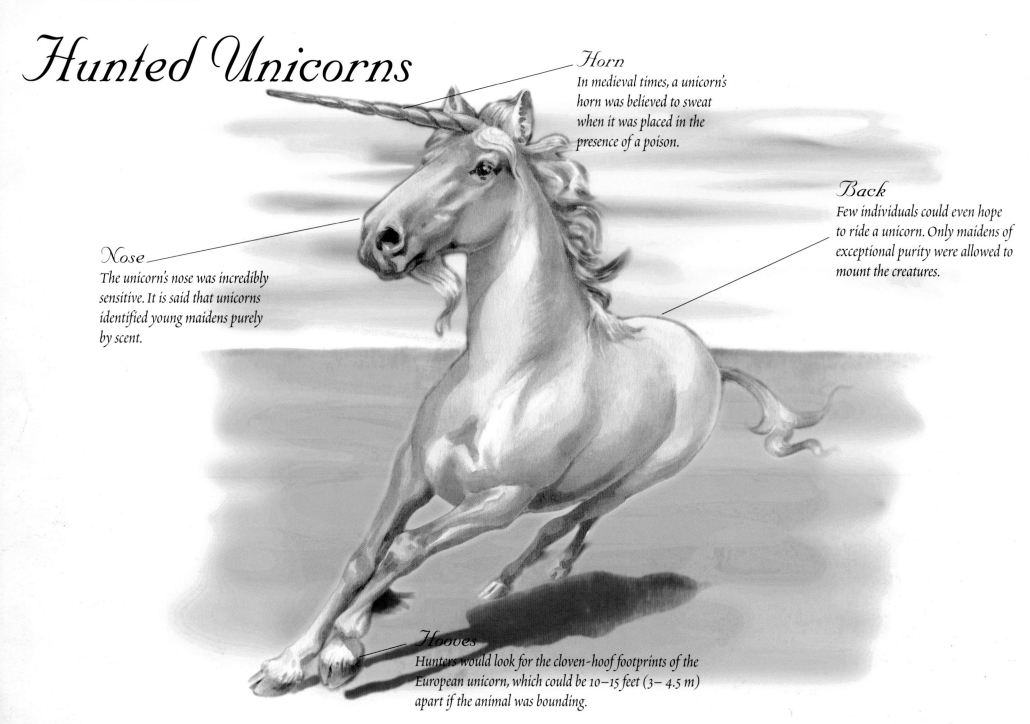

Horn
In medieval times, a unicorn's horn was believed to sweat when it was placed in the presence of a poison.

Back
Few individuals could even hope to ride a unicorn. Only maidens of exceptional purity were allowed to mount the creatures.

Nose
The unicorn's nose was incredibly sensitive. It is said that unicorns identified young maidens purely by scent.

Hooves
Hunters would look for the cloven-hoof footprints of the European unicorn, which could be 10–15 feet (3– 4.5 m) apart if the animal was bounding.

UNICORNS HAVE LONG BEEN HUNTED FOR THEIR HORNS, *which are thought to have healing properties. However, unicorns are fast, alert creatures, and hunters quickly found that they needed cunning ways of capturing the animal. During the Middle Ages in Europe, hunters used young girls as lures for the unicorn, the unicorn valuing an embrace from an innocent girl above all else. Not everyone hunted the creature for its horn, however. In medieval France, noble hunters would track down the unicorn in fast, celebratory chases on horses, only to throw a garland of flowers around the animal when they came close.*

ACTUAL SIZE

▶ *IN A MEDIEVAL FOREST, A HUNTER HAS LONG STRUGGLED TO CATCH AN ELUSIVE UNICORN. His luck is about to change, however. The hunter discovers that a small, beautiful unicorn is attracted to his daughter. While she sits in the forest, he watches from a distance. The unicorn appears. Such is the bond between the two that the unicorn allows the girl to cradle its head in her lap. Immediately the hunter springs his trap, rushing in with dogs and capturing the unicorn. He saws off its horn, which he will then sell, because the magical item commands a high price.*

Where in the world?

Unicorns have been hunted worldwide, but the hunting was more of a sport in the forests of Western and Central Europe during the Middle Ages.

WESTERN EUROPE

CENTRAL EUROPE

Did you know?

★ *The Roman writer Pliny described the unicorn in his book* Naturalis Historia. *He also noted that the unicorn "cannot be taken alive."*

★ *A series of medieval tapestries called* The Hunt of the Unicorn (c. 1500 B.C.) *seems to show hunters killing a unicorn and taking it back to their castle. However, at the end of the tapestries the unicorn is shown alive in captivity, suggesting its eternal nature.*

★ *In ancient times, some markets would sell what they claimed were unicorn horns. In fact, the horns were taken from either the narwhal whale or from certain species of antelope.*

European Unicorns

Horn
The European unicorn usually has a pure white horn, but some books and art depict it with a jet-black horn instead.

Hair
The European unicorn's hair was found in its mane and in its tail, although some pictures also show the unicorn with a short, curling beard.

Teeth
The European unicorn was a grazing animal, and had teeth like a horse's that were good for grinding up plant food.

Blood
The blood of the European unicorn was thought to have the power to heal if applied to sick or injured people.

*T*HE EUROPEAN UNICORN IS THE MOST POPULAR TYPE *seen in movies and books. It is usually a pure white animal, about the size of a small horse, with an elegant body and prancing walk. Stories about the European unicorn start well back in history. The Roman emperor Julius Caesar, for example, spoke of the animal living in the dark forests of Germany. Yet it was during the medieval period that the unicorn truly became popular in Europe. The unicorn was used in art to represent purity. Yet unicorns were also symbols of power and hunting, so they appeared on many official crests and coats of arms.*

ACTUAL SIZE

▶ *A MAN DRINKS FROM A PRECIOUS ALICORN. In the medieval imagination, the horn of a unicorn had great magical powers. It could heal the sick, bring longer life, or even be used as a weapon to destroy evil creatures. This man is taking a drink from an alicorn, the life-giving strength of the horn mingling with the wine poured into it. Yet mortal and immortal things are not meant to touch, and many people who acquired alicorns found they brought as many curses as blessings.*

Where in the world?

Reports of unicorns seem to have spread from the Greek and Roman world up into Western and Northern Europe over the course of several hundred years. Germany, France, Italy, and Britain have particularly strong unicorn traditions.

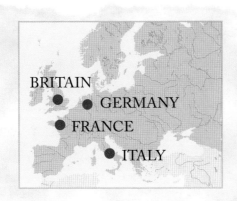

BRITAIN

GERMANY

FRANCE

ITALY

Did you know?

★ *Some medieval European writers wrote that the unicorn could remove poisons from plants or water by making the sign of the Christian cross.*

★ *Between 1550 and 1700 B.C., at least 25 books or long chapters in books were devoted entirely to the discussion of unicorns.*

★ *Many churches around Europe were supposed to have pieces of unicorn horn on display. In the monastery of St. Denis near Paris, for example, the priests listed an alicorn among their possessions. It was 7 feet (2 m) long and weighed a total of 7 pounds (2.6 kg). It was said to have come from a unicorn killed in Persia. This great horn was taken from the monastery in the aftermath of the French Revolution of 1789. The church of St. Mark's in Venice was also famously said to hold two alicorns.*

Noah's Ark

Horn
In Jewish tradition, the unicorn's horn was said to be strong enough to kill an elephant.

Tail
The unicorn's tail suggests how the animal is feeling. If the tail is lifted high, for instance, the animal is alert for danger.

Body
Some species of unicorn are the size of a large horse, whereas others weigh little more than 50 pounds (18.6 kg).

Legs
Unicorns have immensely powerful legs and broad hooves, ideal for swimming.

*T*HE UNICORN IS AN ANCIENT CREATURE *buried deep in time, and many sacred books speak of this magical animal. Some versions of the Bible's Old Testament have several references to unicorns, and there are also legends about unicorns and Noah's ark. According to a Hebrew tale, Noah gathered two of every animal aboard his ark, except for a pair of unicorns—they wanted to play outside rather than go on board the cramped ship. They had their wish, but it was a decision that would cost them their lives. Since then, unicorns have often been associated with childlike qualities.*

ACTUAL SIZE

► TWO UNICORNS PLAY OUTSIDE THE ARK, *even though Noah has begged them to step on board. They refuse to listen, so the ark's doors close, the rain falls, and the waters rise. The unicorns desperately swim for 40 days and nights. Finally, the rains stop, and Noah releases all the ark's birds, which fly away to look for dry land. Many do not find it, but take their rest on the horns of the swimming unicorns. The weight of the birds mounts, and eventually pushes the unicorns beneath the waves.*

Where in the world?

The unicorns of the biblical legend inhabited the lands of the ancient East, which reached from modern-day Egypt through to places such as Iran and Iraq, a region that has been referred to as the "fertile crescent."

ANCIENT
● EAST

Did you know?

★ *In the Ukraine, a country south of Russia, there is a similar flood legend about the unicorns. In this tale, the unicorns refuse to enter the ark because of pride: they boasted that their powers of swimming were so great they did not need to enter the ark. However, the resting birds once again sealed their fate.*

★ *In the King James version of the Bible, an English-language Bible published in England starting in 1611, there are seven references to unicorns in the Old Testament.*

★ *Some believe the unicorns that drowned in the great flood turned into the narwhal, a species of whale that has a single long ivory tusk growing straight out of its head.*

King Arthur

Skull
When the unicorn is born, it naturally does not have a long horn. However, after only a few hours the nub of the horn can be clearly seen.

Horn
The horn on the unicorn was described as being "sharp" and "like a lance."

Eyes
The unicorn expresses many of its feelings through its eyes.

Milk
Unicorn young are fed by drinking their mother's warm, nourishing milk.

*I*N A 14TH-CENTURY STORY, KING ARTHUR'S SHIP *is washed ashore in a strange land. He meets a dwarf who tells him a haunting tale. The dwarf and his wife had been exiled, and his wife died in childbirth. While trying to find shelter for his newborn infant, the dwarf came across a nest full of unicorn fawns. Yet at that moment the unicorn mother returned, the dwarf took fright, and he was separated from his son. However, the unicorn nursed and tended the child as if he were one of her own fawns.*

ACTUAL SIZE

THE DWARF'S SON NESTLES AMONG THE UNICORN FOALS. *Far from being in danger, the child is loved and fed by the unicorn mother, who is attracted to the child's innocence. Because of the unicorn's milk and care, the child eventually grows up to become a giant. The giant son appears at the end of the King Arthur story with the unicorn, and helps refloat the king's ship. Such tales show how the unicorn loves all those who are pure of heart, particularly children.*

Where in the world?

Although the place is not given, King Arthur was probably washed ashore on a remote coastline of Britain or France. Before he was banished, the dwarf worked for the king of Northumbria, a region in northeastern Great Britain.

GREAT BRITAIN

Did you know?

★ *The image of the unicorn has often been used by royalty. In ancient Denmark, the horns of unicorns were used to make royal thrones, although these horns were in fact the long tusks of the narwhal whale.*

★ *It is not common for unicorns to make contact with humans. In the Chinese legends of the kilin, the unicorns live far away from humans in the deep forests. If they come into contact with people, their powers are often weakened.*

★ *Although the dwarf speaks of a nest of fawns, unicorns usually give birth to only a single fawn. This is hidden in lush undergrowth until it is strong enough to walk.*

The Garden of Eden

Size
The Eden unicorn is sometimes shown as being the size of a large horse, whereas other artists depict it only as big as a kid goat.

Tail
The Christian unicorn usually has the tail of a lion. This suggests that the animal is powerful as well as good.

Body
In religious art, the unicorn is often shown as having the body of a powerful stag.

Color
The pure white coat of the unicorn has been used by painters to represent the purity of the Christian life.

*A*LTHOUGH THE BIBLE DOES NOT SPECIFICALLY MENTION unicorns in the Garden of Eden, there are many traditions that give the creature a special place in creation. In one story by writer Nancy Hathaway (The Unicorn, 1981), Adam is given the job of naming all of the animals in the world, and the first creature he names is the unicorn. Adam and Eve spend hours riding around the Garden of Eden on its back. However, Adam and Eve taste the forbidden apple, and the two humans, and the unicorn with them, are banished from the earthly paradise.

ACTUAL SIZE

▶ *ADAM AND EVE SIT TOGETHER IN GOD'S PARADISE*, the beautiful unicorn at their side. Yet their world is about to end. Eve tastes an apple from the forbidden Tree of Knowledge, and Adam joins her. God punishes them by expelling them from paradise, yet gives the unicorn the choice of staying in paradise or going out into the fallen world, where there was death and pain. The unicorn was filled with compassion for its human friends, and stepped through Eden's gates into the hard world beyond.

Where in the world?

The Garden of Eden was most likely located in the ancient region of Mesopotamia in the Middle East, in modern-day Iraq.

IRAQ

Did you know?

★ When the King James version of the Bible was first published in 1611, the translators read the Hebrew word "re'em" as meaning "unicorn." In Job 39:9–12, for example, the writer says "Will the unicorn be willing to serve thee, or abide by thy crib? Canst thou bind the unicorn with his band in the furrow? Or will he harrow the valleys after thee?" The correct translation of "re'em," however, is a large oxlike creature known as an auroch (now extinct).

★ The biblical prophet Daniel is sometimes said to have had visions of unicorns. Another figure from the Bible who may have experienced the unicorn is King David.

Genghis Khan

Size
In the Genghis Khan story, the unicorn was about the size of a small deer.

Mind
The voice that came from the unicorn was probably "spoken" by telepathy, the unicorn shifting the voice from its mind to Khan's. Khan felt that the voice was right next to him, even though the unicorn was some distance away.

Eyes
Khan saw the unicorn's eyes change to those of his father, and then change back to being those of an animal.

Horn
Some accounts say that the horn of the unicorn that faced Khan was red and black in color, not the typical white.

Genghis Khan was a ferocious Mongolian leader who created one of the world's largest empires during the 13th century. Toward his friends he was giving, but anyone who stood in his way was crushed without mercy. Yet according to legend, even he was humbled by the pure unicorn. The story goes that in 1224, Khan took his army to invade India, traveling hundreds of miles through the mountains to the Indian border. On the morning of the planned invasion, however, Khan met a mysterious unicorn who spoke with his father's voice. The unicorn convinced him to call off the entire invasion, and India was saved.

ACTUAL SIZE

▶ THE GREAT WARRIOR GENGHIS KHAN *rises early and rests on a mountaintop, looking down at India. Suddenly, a unicorn stands before him, then walks slowly over and bows three times. Khan feels that the spirit of his father is in the creature. His father has been dead for 50 years, but Khan can see his father's eyes, smell his scent, and feel his emotions. He then hears his father's voice, telling him to go back. Khan listens to the unicorn, turns to his waiting army, and orders them to return to Mongolia.*

Where in the world?

Genghis Khan's Mongol empire covered most of Asia at its height, stretching from the coasts of China through to Eastern Europe.

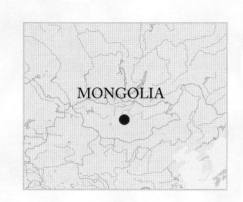

MONGOLIA

Did you know?

★ Although the unicorn is generally an animal associated with peace, it has also been used as a symbol of war. The U.S. 13th Airborne Division, for example, fought hard in World War II and its soldiers wore a shoulder patch featuring a picture of a winged unicorn.

★ In many legends, kings and queens have often sent out warriors and even whole armies to obtain an alicorn. A noble armed with such an item was said to be invincible on the battlefield.

★ The great Roman emperor Julius Caesar believed that unicorns were supposed to live in the forests of Germany. He wrote that the animal was "an ox shaped like a stag, from the middle of whose forehead, between the ears, stands forth a single horn, taller and straighter than the horns we know."

The Lion and the Unicorn

Mane
On the royal coat of arms, the unicorn has a shaggy mane, and the tip of its tail resembles that of a lion.

Neck
In heraldry, the unicorn often has a chain around its neck to show the creature's power and rebellious nature.

Fur
The unicorn's coat is often depicted as being of the brightest white. For this reason, the unicorn has often been used to represent purity.

Hooves
Although the unicorn's horn was its most dangerous weapon against the lion, it could also deliver lethal kicks with its sharp cloven hooves.

Lions and unicorns have a long history together. *In some legends, the unicorn represents the season of spring while the lion evokes summer. In others, the unicorn stands for purity and the lion for violence. A Middle Eastern myth features a celestial lion and unicorn chasing each other through the stars for 28 years, the lion only overcoming the unicorn when the unicorn's horn gets stuck in a tree. In Britain, the lion and the unicorn have been political allegories, and there is even a children's nursery rhyme that begins "The lion and the unicorn were fighting for the crown/The lion beat the unicorn all around the town."*

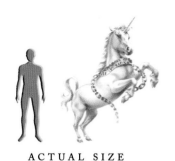

ACTUAL SIZE

DIEU·ET·MON·DROIT

▶ The lion and the unicorn have been part of Britain's heraldry *since the 1300s. Both are featured on the United Kingdom's royal coat of arms and its coins, with the lion representing England and the unicorn representing Scotland (England, Scotland, Wales, and Northern Ireland make up the United Kingdom). On this coat of arms, the unicorn is chained: the English believed that Scotland was like a dangerous animal and had to be controlled.*

Where in the world?

The unicorn and lion came together in British heraldry in 1603, when King James VI of Scotland became King James I of England on the death of Queen Elizabeth I.

● GREAT BRITAIN

Did you know?

★ The Canadian coat of arms is based on the British version, and also features a lion and a unicorn standing either side of a shield. However, the Canadian version shows that the unicorn has broken its chain and is free.

★ Various myths and fables tell that the only way a lion could defeat a unicorn was to stand in front of a tree when the unicorn charged. The lion jumped out of the way at the last minute and the unicorn's horn became stuck in the tree, leaving the animal helpless.

★ In certain traditions, particularly those from Asia, some types of unicorn actually have the bodies or tails of lions, showing their fierce nature.

Harz Mountains Unicorn

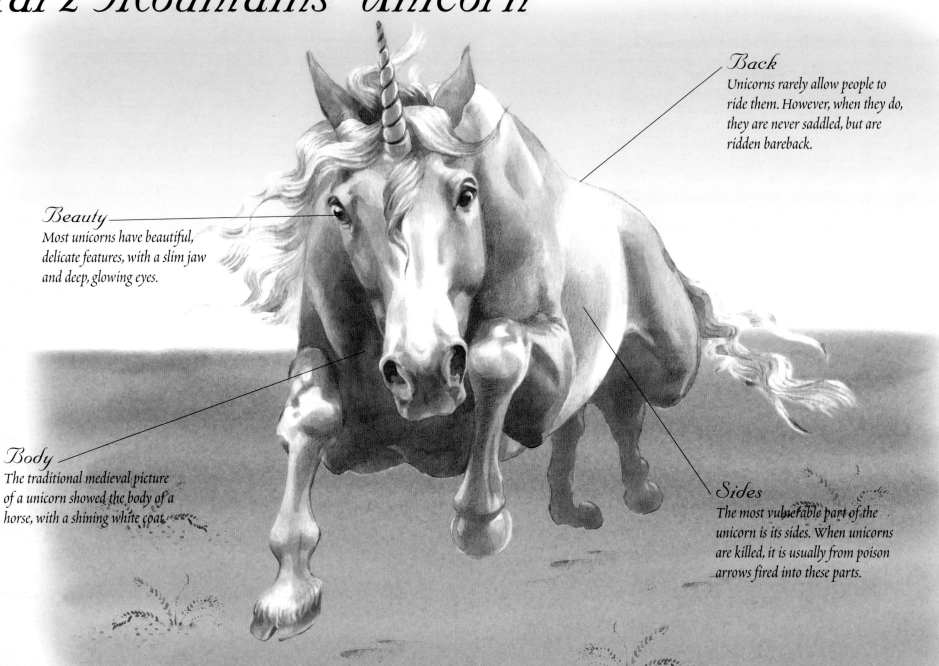

Back
Unicorns rarely allow people to ride them. However, when they do, they are never saddled, but are ridden bareback.

Beauty
Most unicorns have beautiful, delicate features, with a slim jaw and deep, glowing eyes.

Body
The traditional medieval picture of a unicorn showed the body of a horse, with a shining white coat.

Sides
The most vulnerable part of the unicorn is its sides. When unicorns are killed, it is usually from poison arrows fired into these parts.

UNICORNS GENERALLY STAY AWAY FROM PEOPLE, *but sometimes they act as protectors of the pure. A German folktale tells of a mystical old woman who lived in a cave deep in the forests of the Harz Mountains, under the presence of old, natural gods. The woman had powers of healing and fortune-telling, and many people made long journeys into the forest to meet with her. However, the local authorities said that the old woman was a witch. They sent out soldiers to try to capture her and a Christian monk who was to convert her. However, as they closed in on the old woman, a unicorn suddenly appeared and rescued her from the pursuers.*

ACTUAL SIZE

▶ THE SOLDIERS AND THE CHRISTIAN MONK *hunt for the mystical woman of the Harz Mountains. Eventually they spy her, high up in a remote cave, and begin climbing upward. Reaching the cave, they rush toward her. At that point a shining unicorn emerges from the forest and kneels before the woman. She mounts it, and begins to ride off. The monk tries to grab her, but is killed instantly by the combined magical power of the woman and the unicorn.*

Where in the world?

It is said that the magical old woman lived in the Steingrotte Cave near Scharzfeld, in the Harz region. The Harz Mountains run across a large area of northern Germany.

● GERMANY

Did you know?

★ In Germany during the Middle Ages, there was a strange religious cult that worshiped the Virgin Mary. In their rituals they used to called Mary "Maria unicornis," which means "Mary of the Unicorn."

★ Some German monarchs had drinking cups that were supposedly made from alicorns. However, the horns of many other creatures were also described as alicorns, including those of the antelope and the rhinoceros.

★ The alicorn has the magical power to kill as well as heal. One medieval test for deciding whether an alicorn was genuine was to put the horn in a pot with several scorpions. The pot was covered, and after four hours all the scorpions would be dead if the alicorn was real.

Kilins

Horn
The kilin had a particularly majestic horn, with some specimens stretching out to 12 feet (5.6 m) long.

Skin
Rather than having a coat of short fur, some kilin are depicted as being covered in hard green scales.

Body
The body of the kilin can come in many different forms, even a deer, a stag, or a dragon.

Feet
The kilin harms no living thing, and walks so gently that its feet do not even crush blades of grass.

T HE CHINESE KILINS, ALSO CALLED CHILINS, are the oldest of history's unicorns. An ancient Chinese myth tells of a god called P'an Kua who created the heavens and Earth out of chaos. Four animals helped him—a dragon, a phoenix, a tortoise, and a unicorn—and after his work was done, the unicorn disappeared into the dark forests to live. Since then, the unicorn, which can exist for 1,000 years, has been an animal of good omen. Chinese legend has it that the Emperor Fu Hsi, around the year 2900 B.C., saw a magical kilin rise out of the Yellow River and give him the symbols that eventually laid the foundations of Chinese writing.

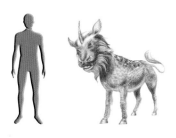

ACTUAL SIZE

▶ A MAGICAL KILIN PULLS A FLAMING CHARIOT, both powerful symbols in ancient and modern Chinese society. This unicorn has the head of a goat, a dragon's body, and a lion's tail. Unicorns have appeared to many Chinese royals. Emperor Huang-Ti, for example, saw the creature wandering around his palace in 2697 B.C., and again at his death when the unicorn carried his soul to heaven. The kilin has been regarded as a symbol of good fortune, appearing in times of peace and prosperity.

Where in the world?

The kilin traditionally inhabits the forests of China, but it also appears to people in glades, around rivers, and sometimes even in palaces.

CHINA ●

Did you know?

★ The symbols given to Fu Hsi are known as the Pa Kua, or eight trigrams. These are eight symbols made up of three horizontal lines each, the lines being either solid or broken in half.

★ Following the unicorn's appearance to Huang-Ti, legend says that the emperor gave many blessings to the Chinese people, including the invention of musical instruments and the ending of tribal wars.

★ It is said that a unicorn appeared in the 6th century B.C. to the mother of Confucius, the Chinese philosopher, and gave her a message telling of the forthcoming birth of her great son.

★ The last of the Chinese emperors to see the kilin was Wu Ti (140–87 B.C.), who honored the creature by building a dedicated unicorn room in his palace.

Karkadann

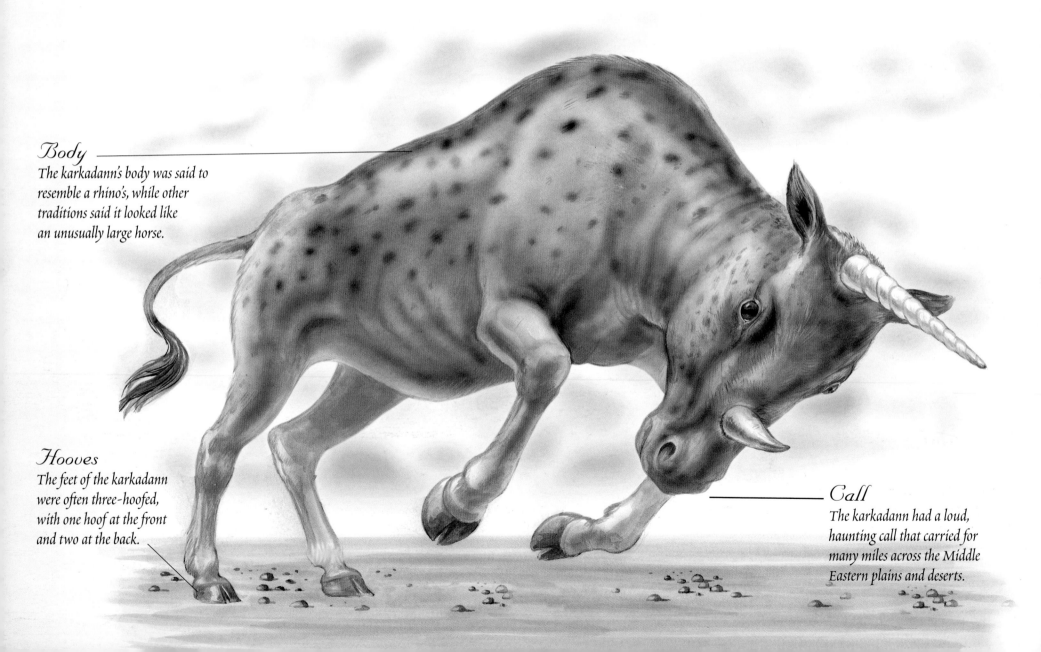

Body
The karkadann's body was said to resemble a rhino's, while other traditions said it looked like an unusually large horse.

Hooves
The feet of the karkadann were often three-hoofed, with one hoof at the front and two at the back.

Call
The karkadann had a loud, haunting call that carried for many miles across the Middle Eastern plains and deserts.

THE MIDDLE EASTERN UNICORN IS VERY DIFFERENT *from those of Europe and other parts of the world. Known as the karkadann, it is said to have lived in India, throughout Persia, and even across North Africa, and was noted for its violent strength and fearsome aggression. Yet it was also a creature that could bestow blessings. Any water touched by the unicorn's horn was instantly purified, and if there were any female creatures in the water they would become mothers. Because of its powers, the unicorn is regarded by many cultures in the Middle East as a good symbol to put on lucky charms, particularly for women.*

ACTUAL SIZE

THE HORN OF THE KARKADANN HAS LONG BEEN KNOWN FOR ITS SPECIAL POWERS. *It was sought for its ability to destroy lethal poisons or to kill poisonous creatures. Tradition has it that one way to tell if a horn was that from a karkadann involved placing it in a vessel with several snakes, spiders, or scorpions. If the horn was real, after only a few minutes the creatures would be dead. Anyone bitten by such creatures might be saved if they were wearing a unicorn symbol as a lucky charm.*

Where in the world?

The karkadann lived across what we today call the Middle East, from Egypt in the west through to northern India in the east.

MIDDLE EAST

Did you know?

★ One story tells of a battle in which a karkadann killed an elephant by stabbing it with its great horn. The dying elephant collapsed on top of the unicorn, and the two creatures died together. At that moment the Roc, a huge mythical bird, swooped down, picked up the two bodies, and took them to its nest to feed its chicks.

★ Unlike European unicorns, the Arabic unicorn liked all women, not just maidens.

★ The ancient warrior Alexander the Great was thought to be able to control a ferocious animal he called Bucephalus. Most people say this was a horse, but some say it was a unicorn with the head of a lion.

★ The only creature that could tame the karkadann was the dove. The unicorn so loved the dove's call that it would wait under a tree or dove's nest for one of the birds to flutter down and land on its horn.

Unicorns as Healers

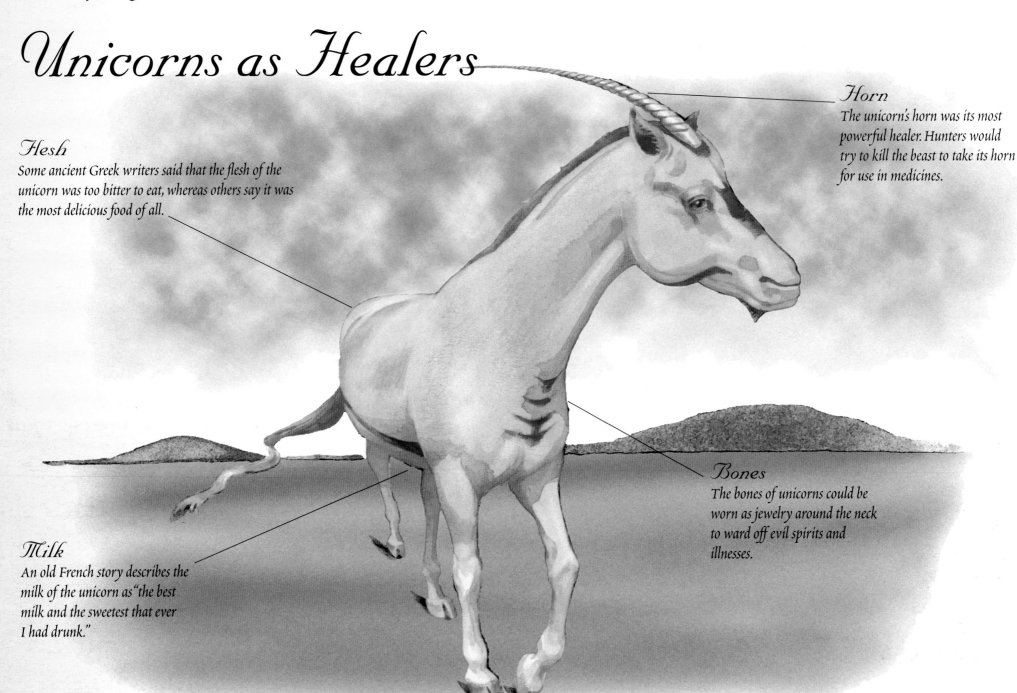

Horn
The unicorn's horn was its most powerful healer. Hunters would try to kill the beast to take its horn for use in medicines.

Flesh
Some ancient Greek writers said that the flesh of the unicorn was too bitter to eat, whereas others say it was the most delicious food of all.

Bones
The bones of unicorns could be worn as jewelry around the neck to ward off evil spirits and illnesses.

Milk
An old French story describes the milk of the unicorn as "the best milk and the sweetest that ever I had drunk."

THE UNICORN HAS TRADITIONALLY BEEN SEEN AS A HEALER, *both of the body and of the mind. Its horn has long been said to have magical healing properties, particularly in stopping the lethal effects of poisons. Drinking unicorn milk could also, it was told, cure diseases or help women struggling to become mothers finally to have a baby. People who were injured would often find that simply touching a unicorn, or handling one of its horns, helped their wounds to heal. In many European and Arabian legends it was believed that someone who was possessed by evil spirits would be made clean again by eating unicorn flesh.*

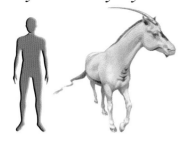

ACTUAL SIZE

▶ A WOMAN GRINDS UP UNICORN HORN IN A PESTLE, *while two other alicorns sit on the shelf behind her, ready for use. The powdered horn would be mixed with water or wine, or placed into a balm, and used as a healing potion. There was a problem with unicorn magic, however. Taking the parts of the unicorn could heal a person's illness, but killing or injuring the unicorn meant committing an evil act. The death of the unicorn might disrupt the natural order, and the hunter would often bring punishment upon himself for killing something of such purity.*

Where in the world?

Healing unicorn stories come from all over the world, but particularly Europe, the Middle East, India, and China. The stories take the form of written text or stories spoken out loud and passed on through generations.

WORLDWIDE

Did you know?

★ The numerous parts of a unicorn supposed to have healing abilities include the horn, the hair, the unicorn's milk and meat, the hooves, and, in the case of some Chinese and Japanese unicorns, the scales covering its body.

★ The unicorn often has been used to represent the harmony of the universe. A royal English verse from the 17th century sees the unicorn in terms of the moon: "The Lion-sun flies from the rising/Unicorn-moon and hides behind the/Tree or Grove of the Underworld;/the Moon pursues, and, sinking in/her turn, is sun slain."

★ Conrad Gessner, a Swiss scientist who lived from 1516 to 1565, said that unicorn horn "is useful and beneficial against epilepsy, pestilential fever, rabies, proliferation and infection of other animals and vermin, and against worms within the body from which children faint."

Harry Potter and Unicorns

Mane
The unicorn's mane is "pearly white," with each strand of hair a pure shimmering color.

Hair
The unicorn's hair is collected for its magical powers, and then used in potions and as the core of magic wands.

Coat
Unicorns are described by Harry as being brilliantly white.

Blood
Unicorn blood in Harry Potter novels is a bright, silvery color. The blood can heal illness and wounds, but also brings a cursed life to those who drink it.

H ARRY POTTER'S WORLD IS STEEPED IN MAGIC, *both light and dark, and the unicorn is a creature of intense power within that world. Harry has a glimpse of unicorn magic when he goes to buy his very first wand. The shopkeeper, Mr. Ollivander, tells Harry, "Every Ollivander wand has a core of a potent magical substance," one of those substances being unicorn hair. The fact that every unicorn has different magical powers means that "No two Ollivander wands are the same." Unicorns appear several times in the Harry Potter novels, and are usually described as being a brilliant white color, as if they are radiating light.*

ACTUAL SIZE

HARRY'S ENCOUNTERS WITH UNICORNS ARE NOT ALWAYS HAPPY. *Harry is in the forest with Hagrid following a trail of unicorn blood, which is silver-colored. They come across a dead unicorn, with a cloaked figure drinking the animal's blood. A centaur tells Harry that killing a unicorn is a hideous crime, and that drinking its blood "will keep you alive, even if you are an inch from death," but that the person who does so will live "a cursed life."*

Where in the world?

The Harry Potter stories are set in England, although the world of magic and wizardry sits alongside normal everyday life. Nonmagical people are unable to see this other world.

● ENGLAND

Did you know?

★ *A German legend from the Middle Ages tells of a king who can save his badly-injured son only by giving him the blood of a unicorn. The king manages to lure a unicorn into the open with a beautiful maiden, hunts it down with four dogs, and takes its blood for his son. The blood immediately cures the young man.*

★ *A traveler named Vincent Leblanc journeyed through India and the Far East in the 16th century. He said that the unicorns that lived in the tropical forests and jungles lived their lives hunted by huge serpents. Apparently the sweet, delicious smell of the unicorn's blood drove the serpents wild with hunger. Leblanc also said that if a unicorn was injured, hunters would collect the blood in a box as a present for their king.*

Jewel

Horn
Jewel's blue horn is a powerful weapon. In one battle he kills two enemy warriors with it.

Legs
Jewel has an incredibly fast gallop, one which "would have carried him out of sight in a few moments."

Chain
Jewel is sometimes seen wearing a chain around his great neck, a piece of jewelry that seems to give him royal status.

*T*HE LAST BATTLE *is the final book in C.S. Lewis' famous* The Chronicles of Narnia. *Like all the books in the series,* The Last Battle *is a religious allegory—it presents a Christian message through a mythical tale. The book explores the great battles between the good kingdom of Narnia, led by King Tirian, and the evil kingdom of the Calormenes. Jewel the unicorn is King Tirian's friend and his loyal protector.*

Jill, one of the humans who ventures into Narnia, describes him as "the shiningest, delicatest, most graceful creature she had ever met ... you would hardly have believed how fierce and terrible he could be in battle."

ACTUAL SIZE

▶ JEWEL IS A POWERFUL AND UNUSUALLY BEAUTIFUL CREATURE, *and although he is a warrior horse, no one in the kingdom of Narnia is allowed to ride him into war, not even the king. Lewis describes Jewel as a majestic animal: a "lordly beast stood close beside the King's chair with its neck bent round, polishing its blue horn against the creamy whiteness of its flank." At the end of the book, Jewel dies in the war against the Calormenes, but his spirit is welcomed into a heavenlike New Narnia.*

Where in the world?

The action takes place in a fantasy world called Narnia, a vast land covered in mountains, forests, and marshland. The human characters in the book, however, come from England, originally from London.

● ENGLAND

Did you know?

★ *In Narnia, animals are divided into talking animals and nontalking animals. Jewel the unicorn is one of the talking animals, and he often stands by the side of the king's throne in conversation.*

★ *Legends of the unicorn usually do not give the creature the power of speech. However, many stories do suggest that the unicorn can pass over its thoughts and feelings to the person who sees it.*

★ *Jewel's horn is described as blue in color. In other stories of unicorns we often find colored horns. The ancient Greek doctor Ctesias, who lived 2,400 years ago, wrote that the Indian unicorn had "a single horn that was bright red at the top, black in the middle, and white at the bottom."*

Alice and the Unicorn

Head
The unicorn's head is very large in proportion to the rest of its body, and it is shaped like that of a horse figure on a chessboard.

Voice
Lewis Carroll's unicorn can talk, and it speaks in an excitable and confident manner.

Shoes
The unicorn is sometimes shown wearing a pair of fine shoes, much like those worn by an English gent of the 17th century.

*I*N LEWIS CARROLL'S TALE, *Alice passes through a mirror and enters a world of absurd creatures. Alice witnesses a particularly unusual scene: a lion and a unicorn locked in battle. Both creatures later talk to Alice, and the unicorn says he thought that children were just a myth. Alice and the unicorn make a pact: "Alice could not help her lips curling up into a smile as she began: 'Do you know, I always thought Unicorns were fabulous monsters, too! I never saw one alive before!' 'Well, now that we have seen each other,' said the Unicorn, 'if you'll believe in me, I'll believe in you. Is that a bargain?'"*

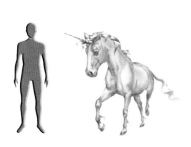

ACTUAL SIZE

▶ *ALICE SEES MANY STRANGE THINGS THROUGH THE LOOKING GLASS. On one occasion, she meets the White King, who takes her to see a memorable event. "Alice had no more breath for talking, so they trotted on in silence, till they came in sight of a great crowd, in the middle of which the Lion and Unicorn were fighting." The prize of this strange fight, which is something like a professional wrestling or boxing match, is the king's crown (or so the lion and unicorn seem to think).*

Where in the world?

Lewis Carroll's tale is set in a magical world on the other side of a mirror, although Alice herself lives somewhere in England.

● ENGLAND

Did you know?

★ *The original pictures for Carroll's book were drawn by the illustrator John Tenniel. Tenniel also drew cartoons for a British satirical magazine called* Punch, *and his lion and unicorn look much like the pictures he did of the politicians William Gladstone and his opponent Benjamin Disraeli.*

★ *Gladstone and Disraeli both became prime minister of Britain during their lifetimes. That could be why Carroll's lion and unicorn battle over the crown.*

The Last Unicorn

Horn
This unicorn is a classic European unicorn, with a straight alicorn rising from the center of her forehead in a spiral pattern.

Magic
The unicorn has powers of magic, mostly confined within the alicorn. The unicorn uses the alicorn to break open padlocks and deliver electriclike shocks.

Coat
The unicorn's coat is the purest white from top to bottom.

Eyes
The unicorn has crystalline blue eyes. When the unicorn is turned into a human, the eyes are the only part of the unicorn that seem left.

*T*HE LAST UNICORN, *a novel by Peter S. Beagle and a subsequent movie, explores the incredible journey of one lone unicorn to find out if she really is the last of her kind. On her journey she discovers that the sinister King Haggard, a royal who wanted to imprison all unicorns for his own pleasure, had a mighty red bull monster drive all unicorns into the sea around his castle, where the creatures remain trapped. The unicorn is nearly killed by the red bull, but she is saved when her companion, Schmendrick the magician, changes her into a mortal woman, whom he calls Amalthea.*

ACTUAL SIZE

▶ *THE UNICORNS MUST FIGHT EVIL IF THEY ARE TO BE FREED. Amalthea falls in love with Haggard's son, Lir, but Schmendrick manages to turn her back into a unicorn. Lir is killed protecting her from the red bull, at which point the unicorn fights back and drives the red bull into the sea. Now all the unicorns of the sea return and help destroy the red bull, and order is once again restored to the world. The unicorn returns to her old life, but she will always remember her experience of being mortal, and especially of being in love with another human.*

Where in the world?

The Last Unicorn *is set in a mythical land of forests, with King Haggard's castle casting the only dark shadow. The castle is eventually destroyed.*

KING HAGGARD'S CASTLE

SEA OF UNICORNS

Did you know?

★ *At the opening of the movie, there are scenes based on the famous 15th-century "Hunt of the Unicorn" tapestries. These tapestries also can be seen hanging in Haggard's castle.*

★ *In* The Last Unicorn, *the alicorn can be seen only by gifted people. As the human Amalthea falls in love with Lir, she herself starts to lose the ability to identify her own kind.*

★ *Unicorns must, on the whole, stay away from mortal creatures to preserve their own immortal natures.*

★ *Most traditions see unicorns as solitary creatures. The only time they live with other unicorns is when a male and female pair to produce young unicorns.*

Unicorns in Legend

Alicorn
When removed, the unicorn's alicorn can be used as a weapon, shooting out destructive bolts of energy.

Body
The unicorn is an immortal creature in Legend, but its body is still not strong enough to resist the poison dart fired by one of the Lord of Darkness' evil goblins.

Legs
The unicorn is one of the fastest creatures in the forest of Legend, although no person is allowed to ride the creature.

Mane
The Legend unicorns have simple, flowing manes of white horses, which match their perfectly white bodies.

L EGEND IS A TALE OF HOW **mortal humans and immortal unicorns must keep apart. A forest dweller, Jack, takes the beautiful Princess Lily to see the world's last pair of unicorns.** She touches one of the unicorns, however, and unintentionally draws it into a trap sprung by the goblins of the evil Lord of Darkness. The unicorn is killed, and the goblins take the alicorn back to their lord while the forest plunges into a dark winter. If the Lord of Darkness can get the second alicorn, his age of darkness will last forever. Lily and the second unicorn are also captured, and imprisoned in the Lord's Tree of Darkness.

ACTUAL SIZE

▶ IT IS LILY'S ATTEMPT TO TOUCH A UNICORN THAT BRINGS DISASTER ON HER KINGDOM. *Legend delivers a warning to humans about unicorns. People are drawn to the purity and beauty of unicorns, but they have to be kept separate. Unicorns also keep the order of Legend's world: "As long as they are on the earth, evil can never harm the pure of heart," one of the fairies tells Jack. Jack and a group of fairies manage to rescue Lily and the unicorn and destroy the evil lord.*

Where in the world?

The world of Legend is a seemingly endless forest. Only the Tree of Darkness, the home of the Lord of Darkness, blights the beauty of the natural world.

JACK'S FOREST

Did you know?

★ *Legend* clearly shows how the unicorns represent good against the powers of evil. In some medieval religious images, the unicorn is often used as a symbol of the power of Christ against that of Satan.

★ The ancient church leader Tertullian (A.D. 155–230) was one of the first people in the Roman Empire to say that the unicorn represented the purity of Christ. However, Tertullian also sees in the unicorn's alicorn the wrath of God against evildoers.

★ Unicorns have appeared in dozens of different movies and television programs. These include unlikely programs such as The Simpsons (where the unicorn is called "Gary") and Mighty Morphin' Power Rangers.

Nico

Hearing
A unicorn's hearing is unusually sensitive. When Nico's mother is killed by a cougar, Nico can hear her distress calls from miles away.

Horn
The horn on Nico's head begins to grow very quickly. Within minutes of him being born, his horn is already 1 inch (2.5 cm) long.

Legs
The enormous power in Nico's legs helps him cross huge distances in a single leap, even with a human on his back.

Hooves
Nico's hooves are more like those of a horse than of a goat. He uses them as powerful weapons when threatened by a mountain lion.

*I*N FRANK SACKS' NOVEL NICO THE UNICORN, *a young boy called Billy is having a tough life. He lost his father in a car accident, and he was left crippled by the accident. However, his life changes forever when a pony bought at a circus gives birth to a unicorn, which Billy calls Nico. As the unicorn grows, new blessings come into Billy's life. The land on which the unicorn lives grows lush and beautiful. Animals from all around—including coyotes, squirrels, and birds—gather to Billy and seem to worship him. Problems begin, however, when the press finds out about the unicorn. They gather around Billy's home, threatening his new way of life.*

ACTUAL SIZE

► BILLY MAKES HIS ESCAPE. *The newspaper and TV reporters chase Nico, with Billy riding on his back. Nico makes huge leaps through the air as they flee, at one point jumping over a ravine that is 100 feet (30m) wide and 500 feet (152 m) deep. After a long chase, Billy and Nico escape. They go through a winding cave that takes them into the Garden of Eden, where Billy's leg is cured. Billy learns the lesson that paradise is there for him, Nico, and all creatures that are "true of heart and to each other."*

Where in the world?

The story is set in the rocky, arid state of Arizona in the United States. Eden is found through a passageway cut into a huge granite cliff.

ARIZONA ●

Did you know?

★ *There are several traditions and legends from history about unicorns being kept as pets. A Persian king, for example, was said to have a tame unicorn in his garden at his palace at Samarkand.*

★ *The unicorn has long been associated with magic spells, particularly regarding the use of its horn. In the medieval period, there were several tests to find out whether a horn was from a unicorn. If the horn was placed in water, it was said that the water would appear to boil. Other theories said that if a spider was placed on the floor, and a circle drawn around it with an alicorn, the spider would not be able to cross the invisible circle and would starve to death.*

Lightfoot

Mane
When Cara sees Lightfoot, she says, "Mane and tail seemed spun of silver cloud and moonlight."

Horn
Lightfoot's horn grows up to 3 feet (0.9 m) long, and seems to glow from the inside.

Skin
The skin of the unicorns seems to become thinner with age. Lightfoot says that the Queen "is thinning now. Sometimes you can see right through her."

Hooves
Lightfoot's hooves are described as "cloven, like a goat's, rather than solid like those of a horse."

*I*NTO THE LAND OF UNICORNS *is a novel by Bruce Colville, part of his Unicorn Chronicles. It tells the tale of a girl called Cara, who is swept into a magical land called Luster, ruled by unicorns and inhabited by many strange creatures. Guided by a friendly unicorn called Lightfoot, Cara discovers that her own father, whom she thought was dead, is actually a hunter of unicorns. Even so, Cara defends the unicorns, which she recognizes as creatures of great purity and kindness. The unicorns of Luster have healing powers in their alicorns. When Cara injures herself, Lightfoot pierces the wound with his horn and the flesh miraculously stitches back together.*

ACTUAL SIZE

▶ CARA FALLS FROM A CHURCH TOWER, BUT LANDS IN LUSTER, UNHURT. *There she meets Lightfoot, who can speak to her using magical words and feelings. Lightfoot can also see into Cara's thoughts and emotions, but says his power cannot heal wounds of the mind. Cara gets to meet the queen unicorn, Arabella Skydancer, one of the oldest of her kind. The book shows how unicorns bond with humans as long as people's intentions are good.*

Where in the world?

Cara falls into the world of Luster after her grandmother gives her a magical amulet. Pursued by the unicorn hunter, Cara jumps from a church tower while clutching the amulet after chanting, "Luster, bring me home...."

Luster

Did you know?

★ *Images of unicorns were often used on amulets to ward away evil spirits or bring good luck. In places as far apart as Italy and China, single unicorn horns are found carved into the woodwork around house doors. In the ancient Middle East unicornlike figures were buried under the floor of a house to bring good fortune.*

★ *During the 18th century in England, there was a curious book by Thomas Boreman called* A Description of Three Hundred Animals, viz. Beasts, Birds, Fishes, Serpents, and Insects, With a Particular Account of the Whale-Fishery. *One animal in the book is the unicorn, of which he says, "Great Virtues are attributed to it, in expelling of Poison, and curing of several Diseases. He is not a Beast of prey."*

★ *European travelers to India in the 16th century discovered that many Indian queens wore bracelets that they claimed were made from unicorn bone.*

Allegra

Mouth
Unicorns, like horses, are plant eaters. In the Ardet Forest, Allegra ate plants such as strawberries, raspberries, and wild asparagus.

Voice
One of Allegra's magical gifts was the power of speech, which is why she was able to make Arianna and King Orlando understand the meaning of the forest.

Tail
While many unicorns are depicted with the tail of a lion, Allegra has a bushy tail like that of a horse.

Color
Allegra's pure white color made it hard for her to hide from the hunters in the summer forest. She smeared herself with mud for camouflage.

THE DRAGON AND THE UNICORN, *a picture novel by Lynne Cherry, is the story of how a unicorn teaches human beings to love nature. The unicorn, called Allegra, lives in harmony with her friend, the dragon Valerio, in a beautiful forest. Their peace is shattered when a king called Orlando brings humans into the forest, who begin to slash down the trees to make a fortress. King Orlando has also heard tales about the power of the unicorn's horn, and so sends hunters out to attempt to kill the unicorn and also her protector Valerio. One day, however, the king's young daughter Arianna wanders into the forest and meets Allegra and Valerio.*

ACTUAL SIZE

▶ WHEN ARIANNA MEETS ALLEGRA AND VALERIO, *she begins a journey of discovery. Allegra teaches her about the beauty and age of the forest. The king, however, sick with worry for his child, goes on his own into the forest to look for her, and on the way discovers for himself the beauty of the natural world. He eventually finds Arianna, who takes him to meet Allegra and Valerio. The king sees his errors, and declares, "We will learn to love and respect this forest."*

Where in the world?

The Dragon and the Unicorn is set in the mythical Ardet Forest. It is a place of great natural beauty and harmony, full of wonderful creatures, delicate flowers, and massive trees.

ARDET FOREST

Did you know?

★ *Unicorns have always had a strong connection with the natural environment. There are reports of paintings of unicorns on cave walls in parts of southern Africa, which date from the earliest days of human existence.*

★ *Some scientists have said that unicorns used to exist in the tropical rain forests of South America, but they were hunted to extinction around 7,000 years ago.*

★ *In 1633, in a mountainous and forested part of Germany, a unicorn skeleton was supposedly found. The skeleton was examined by several great scientists and thinkers of the day, and some were convinced that the remains were indeed from a true unicorn.*

Index